I HATE PHP

A Beginner's Guide to PHP and MySQL PLR Version

Copyright Your Site

The author nor the publisher can be held liable for any loss incurred by the advice given in the following publication. You agree to hold the author, publisher, and any/all subsidiaries harmless in the event of loss or harm. We make no guarantee of performance or income gained from the information within this publication. You do not have redistribution rights of any kind for this publication, in any form, be it physical or electronic, unless specifically granted by the author and/or publisher.

OK, I don't *REALLY* hate PHP, but there have been days I strongly dislike it. Thank you for purchasing this guide to PHP and MySQL. I hope you get some enjoyment out of it, and learn a few things!

First of all, my background and why this book came to be...

Most PHP/MySQL books on the market that I have read were not written for the novice. To be honest, even I struggled with "PHP For Dummies", although I've been working with HTML and another programming environment, ColdFusion, for years. So, WHY was PHP so hard for me? I think it was a number of things, but most of all because with HTML and ColdFusion experience, I was used to a TAG based language. For everything there was a tag, like this:

`<cfoutput>`

...which is a ColdFusion tag to output processed information. PHP is not based on tags like that. No, PHP more resembles a (ugh) Programming Language. If you are intimidated by that, never fear - I'm going to do my best to explain the examples in plain english!

So, who is this book for?

This book is for the lonely people who can't get a da...hold on...wrong book..."I Hate PHP" is for webmasters and designers who have always wondered what PHP could do for *them;* someone who wants to "do" some PHP and not outsource it. It is best to be familiar with HTML and writing / deciphering HTML code. You don't need to be a top-notch "I do it all in Notepad" kinda person - just being able to open up a text editor and understand the code is enough. Copy / Paste knowledge is helpful too.

Unlike other PHP books on the market, we are *not* going to attempt to cover every single facet of the Wide World Of PHP Language. No, we want to grasp the basics of the language, get familiar with it, and get some real-life examples...not have the whole thing shoved down our throat!

You'll find that throughout this book, my odd sense of humor may shine through a little bit. You might not find that web programming is the most exciting thing on the planet. Well, I don't either, so I tried to make it interesting and easy to read.

More Places To Learn

At the end of the book, we'll include some links to other websites and products that will help you on your journey to PHP mastery. We're not endorsing them...just providing them. You must walk the path, young grasshopper.

Presentation

The examples in this book are presented in 3 levels - *The Easy Stuff, The Not So Easy Stuff, and Oh Man Not MySQL!*

The Easy Stuff consists of common PHP commands you can use on just about any site you build. *The Not So Easy Stuff* is code that is a little more difficult to grasp, but you might still want to use it. *Oh Man Not MySQL!* will cover - you guessed it - how to connect to a MySQL database and do basic things, like writing to it and retrieving information.

And now, without futher ado....

Section 1:

The Easy Stuff

Covering ECHO, STRING, DATE, VARIABLES, INCLUDE, REQURE, and HEADER

Before we get into learning how to use PHP, we need to briefly explore what PHP is...but I'm not going to go into some long drawn out history of PHP and why it's here. Also, it is good to be familiar with HTML before you proceed, as you will need to be able to copy and paste code in web pages.

In the world of the wide web, there are two general types of coding languages: "Server side" and "Client side". This means that one type is run, or interpreted, on the web server itself, and the other is run in your web browser.

> **Think of it this way...**
> *Server side:* You order a sandwich at a restaurant. It comes to you already prepared and ready to eat.
> *Client side:* You order a sandwich at a restaurant. Individual sandwich parts (bread, meat, lettuce, tomatoes, condiments) are delivered to you separately and you have to assemble them before you eat.

PHP is a Server side language. All of the processing is done on the web server itself, and the result is delivered to your web browser as HTML (which, by the way, is a Client side language). Your web server must also have PHP installed in order for it to work! Most web hosting providers have PHP installed, so if you are in doubt, simply ask them.

> **Things To Note:**
> There are three things that need to happen before the web server correctly runs a PHP command.
>
> **1.** The filename must be "file.php" instead of the usual "file.htm" or "file.html". If it has the HTM or HTML extension, the PHP engine on the web server will ignore it. *(There are exceptions to this, but we won't go into them right now.)*
>
> **2.** The PHP code must be within the <?php and ?> tags. If it is not, the PHP engine on the web server will ignore it.
>
> **3.** Each PHP line must end with a Semicolon. If it does not, you're going to get some cryptic error messages.

Now, Let's Code!

We're going to tackle the basics to start with. Getting PHP to write things to the web browser, what variables are and how to use them...examples you can use in just about every web page you create.

Let's start with the most basic one.

The PHP Echo command
We're going to tell PHP to output something to the screen. Keep in mind that PHP can be used in conjunction with HTML, but we are not showing the code in this example, to keep it simple:

```
<?php echo 'Creamy Bagels'; ?>
```

(I hate the "Hello World" sample that every other book in the world uses, so I'm using "Creamy Bagels" instead.)

Let's dissect the command example bit by bit, shall we? It helps to do this when you are looking at a LOT of PHP code...because, trust me, it can look like a jumbled blurry mess sometimes if you don't take it piece by piece! Next page, please, if you will...

<?php - tells the server to process this as php code...

echo "Creamy Bagels" ; - tells the server to write what's in the quotes to the screen, and that the semicolon is ending this particular command...

?> - tells the webserver, "OK, I'm done with PHP for now. Back to regular HTML".

Pretty simple when you look at it that way, yes?

"OK, that's cool..but what if I want to see quotes on my screen?"

This can be done by "escaping" the PHP code for what you want to show up in quotes. Let's use the example from above...

<?php echo 'Creamy Bagels'; ?>

If you wanted to see quotes around Creamy Bagels, you would use the following code instead:

<?php echo "\"Creamy Bagels\""; ?>

Using \" tells PHP that you want a quotation mark to appear. Remember this - we're going to use it later!

Pull some Strings...

In PHP, as a general rule, a String is any line of text contained within quotation marks. You can use either double quotation marks (") or single quotation marks also known as apostrophes (') in a string. Strings could be considered the building blocks of PHP, considering most all data is going to come from what's in a string.

<?php

$double = "quotation marks.";

$single = 'single quotes.';

?>

When using single quotes, you need to "escape" the apostrophe with the slash (just like you would with double quotation marks) if you wish to display it in the output text...

<?php

echo 'wouldn\'t you like a bagel?';

?>

Special commands within strings...

There are some "secret commands" you can use within strings to manipulate the output text:
\n: makes a new line
\r: a carriage return
\t: a tab
\$: shows a dollar sign - remember PHP will be looking for a variable if you want to display a dollar sign and don't use a slash...and throw an ugly error!

Using Variables

A Variable in PHP, simply put, is one thing that means another thing or things - a "container" if you will. It can represent text, numbers, calculations, and more.

Variables are quite powerful, and if you mess 'em up, they'll come get you in the middle of the night.

Declaring a variable is easy. No spaces in the variable name, please - PHP doesn't like that...

<?php

$This_thing = "The Other Thing";

?>

Now before you go off saying "What the heck would I need THAT for?", remember that variables are very useful...especially if you are PHP Include-ing other files (Like the foreshadowing there? Do ya?)

Real World Usage For Variables

Here's an example of how you can use a variable in the real world: show the current date on your website.

```
<?php
$today = date("F j, Y");
echo "$today";
?>
```

This example sets the date command as a variable called "$today", and uses echo to display it on the screen.

March 16, 2007

And now, for a quick tangent...

More about the "DATE" command - it is very versatile and flexible - see the guide below to use it to it's potential!

The DATE command

Expanding on the above example, here are the options for DATE and TIME display:

Time:
a: am or pm
A: AM or PM
g: Hour without leading zeroes (1-12)
G: Hour in military time without leading zeroes (0-23)
h: Hour with leading zeroes (01-12)
H: Hour in military time with leading zeroes (00-23)
i: Minute with leading zeroes (00-59)
s: Seconds with leading zeroes (00-59)

Days:
d: Day of the month with leading zeroes (01-31)
j: Day of the month without leading zeroes (1-31)
D: Day of the week abbreviations (Sun – Sat)
l: Day of the week (Sunday – Saturday)
w: Day of the week without leading zeroes (0-6)
z: Day of the year without leading zeroes (1-365)

Months:
m: Month of the year with leading zeroes (01-12)
n: Month of the year without leading zeroes (1-12)
M: Month abbreviations (Jan – Dec)
F: Month names (January – December)
t: Number of days in the month (28-31)

Years:
L: Displays 1 if it is a leap year, 0 if not
Y: Year in 4-digit format (2006)
y: Year in 2-digit format (06)
Other Date Formats:
r: Full date, including timestamp and timezone offset (O)
U: Number of seconds since the Unix Epoch (Jan. 1, 1970)
O: Offset difference from Greenwich Meridian Time (GMT). 100 = 1 hour, -100 = -1 hour

---

And now...back to Variables!

ECHOing more that one Variable at a time

You can use the ECHO command we learned earlier to display more than one variable at a time. Combining variables can be extremely useful. Take a look at this example...

```
<?php

$phrase1 = "That's No Moon,";

$phrase2 = "It's a Space Station!";

echo "$phrase1 $phrase2";

?>
```

This code example will show up in your web browser like this:

Neat, huh?

That's No Moon, It's a Space Station!

So, you can see where this might be useful, I hope?

You can also echo text and variables in the same statement by putting periods around the variable....like so...

```
<?php

$items = 3;

echo "You have purchased ".$items." items.";

?>
```

You have purchased 3 items.

PHP Includes

A PHP include is used when you want to include the contents of one file inside another...a very useful command!

```
<?php

include('file.inc');

?>
```

Real World Usage for Includes

Let's say you are developing a 5 page website that you might be adding pages to. Your navigation HTML looks like this:

```
<html>
<head>
<title>My Navigation</title>
</head>
<body>
<a href=http://www.mysite.com/index.php>Home</a>
<a href=http://www.mysite.com/products.php>Products</a>
<a href=http://www.mysite.com/articles.php>Articles</a>
<a href=http://www.mysite.com/blog.php>Blog</a>
<a href=http://www.mysite.com/contact.php>Contact Us</a>
</body>
</html>
```

...and this is going to be in every page. Now, when you add a page to your website, you are going to have to change the code on all 5 pages to reflect the new link. This could take several minutes to do...and what if the site expands to 20 pages or more? It's going to be a nightmare!

PHP Includes to the rescue!
Turn the page and watch PHP save our developer from certain doom!

Let's cut the menu link code out of the example above and paste it into a new plain text document (You can use Notepad on Windows or TextEdit on the Mac for this).

```
<a href=http://www.mysite.com/index.php>Home</a>
<a href=http://www.mysite.com/products.php>Products</a>
<a href=http://www.mysite.com/articles.php>Articles</a>
<a href=http://www.mysite.com/blog.php>Blog</a>
<a href=http://www.mysite.com/contact.php>Contact Us</a>
```

Save this text file as navigation.inc. Paste the following in place of where the code was in the original HTML files...

```
<?php
include "navigation.inc" ;
?>
```

Then save the HTML page as a PHP page. Voila! Any time you need to change the menu links, all you have to do is edit one file - the navigation.inc file!

> **A Note on Includes...**
> You don't have to use .inc as the extension for an include - you can include almost any type of file with a PHP include - HTML, PHP, even other URL's! One thing to keep in mind, however...is to strip out all the formatting code from the page you are including from (like the <html> and <body> tags). In other words, only include exactly what you need!

I Require You To Include

In PHP, you can also use the "Require" command in place of Include. The major difference between the two is that using Require will stop the script from running (the page won't load completely) if it cannot find the page that is referenced for inclusion. An Include will allow the page to load, but it will just ignore the included code if it cannot be found.

Now let's mesh it all together in an example!

Imagine this...you are building a website. Your Greatest Undertaking Of A Website. 200 Pages. 400 Articles. Writing Code By Hand. The Titan Of Websites. You want to put advertising on each page (We'll use Google™ AdSense as an example). You also want to test different color themes on the ad code, or change the ads periodically. You are also going to be quite generous and give copies of this website away for others to use.

The questions start filling your mind...how can I easily change the ad colors or format? How can I let other people easily put in their AdSense publisher code?

We'll use Variables and Includes to solve the problem!

Open up 2 blank text documents. The first one is going to be a settings file, the second one is going to be your Ad code.

In the settings file, you are going to want to set variables for things you know you are going to want to change, the main thing being the AdSense publisher code and the ad link colors. So, we'll set the variables as below...

```
<?php

$ad_pub_num = 'pub-0123456789';

$eb_linkcolor = '006699';

?>
```

The variable, $ad_pub_num, now reflects the AdSense publisher tracking code, and the link colors are the HTML color code 006699, which is a dark blue. Save this page as settings.php.

Now, grab your AdSense code snippet from Google...

```
<script type="text/javascript"><!--
google_ad_client = "pub-0123456789";
google_ad_width = 120;
google_ad_height = 600;
google_ad_format = "120x600_as";
google_ad_type = "text_image";
google_ad_channel = "1";
google_color_border = "FFFFFF";
google_color_bg = "FFFFFF";
google_color_link = "006699";
google_color_text = "006699";
google_color_url = "006699";
//--></script>
  <script type="text/javascript"
  src="http://pagead2.googlesyndication.com/pagead/show_ads.js">
</script>
```

And paste it into the other open document...making some changes...

```
<?php echo "
  <script type=\"text/javascript\"><!--
google_ad_client = \"$ad_pub_num\";
google_ad_width = 120;
google_ad_height = 600;
google_ad_format = \"120x600_as\";
google_ad_type = \"text_image\";
google_ad_channel = \"1\";
google_color_border = \"FFFFFF\";
google_color_bg = \"FFFFFF\";
google_color_link = \"$eb_linkcolor\";
google_color_text = \"$eb_linkcolor\";
google_color_url = \"$eb_linkcolor\";
//--></script>
  <script type=\"text/javascript\"
src=\"http://pagead2.googlesyndication.com/pagead/show_ads.js\">
</script>
?>
```

...and save this file as ads.php.

Do you recognize the changes we made? We've told PHP to echo the code to the screen, and put in the variables that we set in the settings.php file. Since we are doing an ECHO, we're displaying the quotation marks in the output with the \" code (That's the way the AdSense snippet works). Now we are ready to call these files from the main web pages!

At the beginning of your content pages, you will want to add this code:

```
<?php

require "settings.php";

?>
```

This tells the page that it requires the contents of Settings.php file to be included. Including this code on each page sets the variables we will use throughout the site.

Now, call the ads in the places you want them:

```
<?php

include "ads.php";

?>
```

This will pull in the code from the ads page we made, including the variables we set, and show those ads wherever you care to place them. So, your ad link colors will appear in a dark blue and the example publisher number - pub-0123456789 - will show up in the ads. Name each one of your content pages as .php instead of .html, and you'll be good to go! If you decide you want to change colors of the ads (or change the AdSense publisher ID code), you only have to make that change in ONE file instead of 200 - the settings.php file!

Redirects using PHP HEADER

You can use PHP to create redirects to other pages or websites. This is quite useful if you do any kind of affiliate marketing and hate the ugly links provided - use the Header command to clean 'em up!

```
<?php

header ('Location: http://linktoredirect.com');

?>
```

When a viewer visits this PHP page in their browser, they will be redirected to the link reflected in the "Location" part of the code. This is a good method to use, since other redirect methods using HTML and Javascript can easily be blocked. Header can be used for other functions, but this is one of the more common uses, so we'll leave it at that for now.

Section One Overview...

While we have not covered the entirety of basic PHP commands, the ones we have covered are among the most common and can be used in almost any web project.

ECHO: Outputs to the screen.
STRING: Content within a PHP command.
VARIABLES: Something equals something else.
DATE: A way to display date/time.
INCLUDE: Pull in the contents of another file.
REQUIRE: Require the contents of another file.
HEADER: Redirects to new file / URL.

And now....for a...

...QUICK QUIZ!!!

1. What is the difference between INCLUDE and REQUIRE?

2. Can we ECHO words with quotation marks? How?

3. What is a VARIABLE used for?

Very good. Now, take a short brain break...then go on to the next section!

Section 2:

The Not-So-Easy Stuff

Covering IF, ELSE, SWITCH, ARRAY, FUNCTIONS, SESSIONS, and COOKIES.

You Made It Past The Basics - Congratulations!

By now, you've got enough PHP knowledge under your belt to add basic PHP functionality in all of your websites. It's pretty cool knowing things that a lot of others don't know, and they'll never be able to find out just by doing a "View Source" on your website (especially since you cant actually SEE PHP code by viewing the source in a browser!)

In this section we are going to cover some more advanced PHP code. Things that you might not use just yet but once you are comfortable with PHP and want to get more out of it, you'll be ready, my young apprentice.

Quick tangent...before we get started here you are going to want to be able to place comments in your code. Why? It's a heck of a lot easier to know why you wrote a specific line of code if you add comments...so you don't come back in 3 months and ask yourself, "Was I drunk when I wrote this code??" Here are some examples of comment codes:

```
<?php

// This is a single comment line

# This is also a single comment line

/* This is a block comment, useful if you are working with a multi-line
comment or are writing a story on your page that you don't want
people to see */

?>
```

You don't have to use semicolons after each line, since the PHP server ignores comments because they aren't actually commands. Now, on to more CODE! (ta-daaaa!)

The IF statement

The IF statement in PHP is very similar to using IF in real life. Like IF you don't set your alarm clock, then you'll be late to work in the morning. IF (and it's friend ELSE) are known as "conditionals".

First off, let's look at how PHP compares values for conditionals. You'll see "operators" in any IF statement:

- == Equal to
- != Not equal to
- < Less than
- \> Greater than
- <= Less than or equal to
- \>= Greater than or equal to

So, a valid IF statement could be illustrated as follows:

```
<?php

if ($variable == "some value") {

echo "Correct";}

?>
```

Expanding on IF with ELSE

You'll most likely want to use IF with ELSE. ELSE gives you the option of doing something ELSE with your PHP script if IF doesn't calculate one way or another. For example, you can have your site display something IF a condition is met (like a password was correct...see below!) or something ELSE if not. (Like a redirect if the password is not!)

Code example...

```php
<?php
$five = '5';
if ($five == '5') {
    echo "You are correct";
} else {
    echo "You are incorrect";
}
?>
```

Real World Usage For If/Else

You could create a simple password protected area using If/Else. A PHP page with a conditional statement could be set up to process an HTML login form. A variable "$password" could be set, and the Header command could be used to redirect on success or failure.

Your HTML page would be a simple form...

```
<form action="login.php" method="post">
<INPUT type="password" name="password">
<input type="submit">
</form>
```

This HTML form will set the variable in the "action" page (named login.php in this example) with the $_POST command (more on this later) and do one of two things: If the password is correct, it will show the desired content. If it is NOT correct, it will redirect to another URL (or page).

Since the action is in PHP, viewing the source in the web browser isn't going to reveal the password.

...And your PHP "Action" page would be an If/Else combined with a Redirect...

```
<?php
if($_POST['password'] == 'some_password'){

echo "
<!---Put your protected HTML content here...-->
";
} else {
header ("location: some_error_page.html");
}
?>
```

...And Voila! A simple way to password protect a page. I wouldn't use this for sensitive stuff (like putting your social security number online) but it's good for a simple, single layer of security.

IF, meet ELSE. ELSE, meet ELSEIF

The IF/ELSE statement is wonderful if you need to check for only one condition. But, what if you need to check for multiple conditions? Like, for instance, IF a truck is a Dodge, do this...ELSE a truck is a Chevy, do this...but what if you need to have options if a truck was a Ford?
In this example, we simply want to see if a truck is a Dodge or not. We can do this with IF / ELSE...

```
<php
$truck = "Chevy";
if($truck == "Dodge"){
      echo "It's Ram Tough!";
} else {
      echo "We'll Be There!";
}
?>
```

Now, if we wanted to see if the truck was a Ford, we'd add the ElseIf statement...

```php
<php
$truck = "Chevy";
if($truck == "Dodge"){
	echo "It's Ram Tough!";
} elseif {$truck == "Ford"}
	echo "Built Ford Tough!";
} else {
	echo "We'll Be There!";
}
?>
```

...And so on. You could continue to use ElseIf to declare other Trucks. One thing to remember about ElseIf is that it can't be used without IF. So what if you have a lot of ElseIf's?? Let's see what's behind the curtain, Bob...

Flip the SWITCH

Sometimes we have to evaluate more than just a few cases, making ElseIf a tad cumbersome (do YOU want to write 20 ElseIf's? I don't!) Enter the more streamlined and efficient SWITCH command. Let's add some more trucks to our list, shall we?

```php
<?php
$truck = "Chevy";
echo "Drive a $truck, <br/>";
switch ($truck){
	case "Dodge":
		echo "Ram Tough!";
		break;
	case "Ford":
		echo "Built Ford Tough!";
		break;
	case "Toyota":
		echo "Got The Guts?";
		break;
	case "Nissan":
		echo "Shift_power";
```

```
            break;
        case "GMC":
            echo "Professional Grade";
            break;
} ?>
```

That looks a little cleaner, don't you think? A tad less clumsy that an equal number of If/Else statements. Make sure when you use Switch to include the "break" statement - it not, the information will be processed until the script "breaks" or ends.

Also, notice that there is no default statement for when we match our condition! We need to add something to Switch - the *default* case.

```
<?php
$truck = "Chevy";
echo "Drive a $truck, <br/>";
switch ($truck){
        case "Dodge":
            echo "Ram Tough!";
            break;
        case "Ford":
            echo "Built Ford Tough!";
            break;
        case "Toyota":
            echo "Got The Guts?";
            break;
        case "Nissan":
            echo "Shift_power";
            break;
        case "GMC":
            echo "Professional Grade";
            break;
        default:
            echo "We'll Be There!";
            break;
} ?>
```

This way, if there are no matching cases, our default is displayed.

ARRAYS

An Array can be thought of as a single variable that stores more than one value. An array uses a *key* to determine what value to reference. So;

$array[key] = value;

Key values start at "0" normally, as PHP likes to number things starting at Zero instead of One. It's a programming thing, I don't know either.

Let's use our truck examples from above, and assign then in an array.

```
<?php
$truck_array[0] = "Toyota";
$truck_array[1] = "Dodge";
$truck_array[2] = "Chevy";
$truck_array[3] = "Ford";
?>
```

And here's how we could output information from the array:

```
<?php
echo "Two great truck makers are "
. $truck_array[0] . " & " .
$truck_array[1];
echo "<br />Two more great truck makers are "
```

Two great truck makers are Toyota & Dodge
Two more great truck makers are Chevy & Ford

```
. $truck_array[2] . " & " . $truck_array[3];
?>
```

Here's is the output result of the above array:

Associative Arrays

An Associative Array is an array in which the keys are associated with values.

```
<?php
$truck["Toyota"] = Tundra;
$truck["Nissan"] = Titan;
$truck["Dodge"] = Ram;
?>
```

A Syntax example using the Associative Array above:

Toyota makes the Tundra
Nissan makes the Titan
Dodge makes the Ram

```
echo "Toyota makes the " .
$truck["Toyota"] . "<br />";
echo "Nissan makes the " .
$truck["Nissan"] . "<br />";
echo "Dodge makes the " . $truck["Dodge"];
```

And, when viewed in a browser...

You may not see the usefulness of the Array and Associative Array right now, but I think (hope) it will come together a little more once we hit the next lesson - LOOPS.

Let's move on!

LOOPS

We all have mundane, repetitive tasks we have to do. You know, like putting stamps on all those holiday greeting cards we send out every year? Well, from a programming angle, PHP can help us ease the workload on repetitive tasks in websites with a LOOP.

The first one we'll discuss is the *WHILE LOOP*. It sounds like a weird carnival ride (I got sick on the While Loop - it was great!) but it is one of the most useful loop functions in PHP.

Logically, it looks like this:

```
while ( this conditional statement is true){
      //do this;
}
```

This isn't real code - just an illustration of how it works. now, here's what happens, step by step:

1. PHP checks the conditional statement. If it is true, move to step 2. If it is false, go to step 4.
2. PHP runs the code contained in the loop.
3. We go back to step 1 and start again, making a LOOP.
4. Once the conditional statement becomes false, the loop exits, and code placed after the loop runs.

Real World Usage for WHILE LOOPS

The Creamy Bagel Company wants to show a pricing matrix on their website for up to a 20 bagel pack. But, since bagels are a valuable commodity, the price fluctuates regularly. You have to change it. You love your job.

Using a While Loop and some HTML, this can happen with relative ease, and you'll only have to change *one* value when the bagel price changes (then charge for 3 hours of work!). Read on...

```
<?php
$bagel_price = 2.15; //This is the price of one bagel
$counter = 1;

echo "<table border=\"1\" align=\"center\">"; //note the escapes for quotes!
echo "<tr><th>Quantity</th>";
echo "<th>Price</th></tr>";
while ( $counter <= 20 ) { //we just set the counter limit at 20
        echo "<tr><td>";
        echo $counter;
        echo "</td><td>";
        echo $bagel_price * $counter; //here we multiply
        echo "</td></tr>";
        $counter = $counter + 1; //here we add 1 to the counter and start again
}
echo "</table>";
?>
```

Quantity	Price
1	2.15
2	4.3
3	6.45
4	8.6
5	10.75
6	12.9
7	15.05
8	17.2
9	19.35
10	21.5
11	23.65
12	25.8
13	27.95
14	30.1
15	32.25
16	34.4
17	36.55
18	38.7
19	40.85
20	43

Our actual Loop code is highlighted in blue above. You'll see that we set the variables $bagel_price and $counter. The $counter variable allows us to create a math function to increment the unit price by 1 each time we loop (see the $counter = $counter + 1 part at the bottom of the loop?)

So, while $counter equals less-than-or-equal-to 20, this loop will function. Once we hit 21, that's it - no more loop!

> **Note on PHP Math functions**
> **+** addition (You can use ++ to increment a value by 1)
> **-** subtraction
> ***** multiplication
> **/** division

Here's what it looks like in a browser...and you can see at-a-glance what 13 bagels will cost you!

The FOR LOOP

The FOR LOOP is very similar to a WHILE LOOP. The difference being a little bit more code is contained in the loop. The FOR LOOP can be a little more compact than a WHILE LOOP. Here's the logic:

```
for ( create a counter; conditional statement; increment the counter){
        do this;
}
```

Let's use our fluctuating bagel cost from above and write this out. Oops - bagels just went up 10 cents!

```
<?php
$bagel_price = 2.25;

echo "<table border=\"1\" align=\"center\">";
echo "<tr><th>Quantity</th>";
echo "<th>Price</th></tr>";
for ( $counter = 1; $counter <= 20; $counter += 1) {
        echo "<tr><td>";
        echo $counter;
        echo "</td><td>";
        echo $bagel_price * $counter;
        echo "</td></tr>";
}
echo "</table>";
?>
```

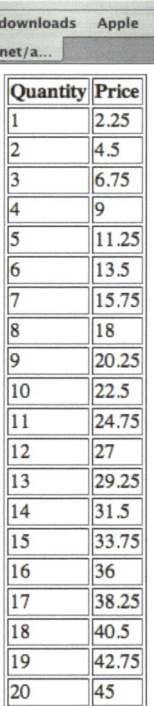

Quantity	Price
1	2.25
2	4.5
3	6.75
4	9
5	11.25
6	13.5
7	15.75
8	18
9	20.25
10	22.5
11	24.75
12	27
13	29.25
14	31.5
15	33.75
16	36
17	38.25
18	40.5
19	42.75
20	45

Once again, the loop is highlighted in blue. You'll notice that the counter is defined inside the loop as opposed to a variable outside.

And..to the right, you'll see the output.

There's one more Loop we're going to cover, isn't this exciting? Hello? Still there?

The FOR EACH Loop

What if you want to loop through an Associative Array? (See? Told you we'd get back to this!) You can use FOR EACH to do this task. Where the WHILE and FOR loops run until an error is encountered, the FOR EACH loop will run through every element in the array.

Let's revisit the associative array we set up with the trucks...

```
<?php
$truck["Toyota"] = Tundra;
$truck["Nissan"] = Titan;
$truck["Dodge"] = Ram;
?>
```

Make: Toyota, Model: Tundra
Make: Nissan, Model: Titan
Make: Dodge, Model: Ram

To loop through the Makers / Models, we'd use this code:

```
<?php
foreach( $truck as $make => $model){
    echo "Make: $make, Model: $model <br />";
}
?>
```

The code is written in a strange way, it isn't obvious how it works. Let's look at it in a simpler way:

$something as $key => $value

So, in english...

FOR each thing in the array, I want to refer to the *key* as $key and the *value* as $value. The operator '=>' indicates the relationship between the key and the value...the key "points" to the value.

I think that's about all we need to cover with Loops. Next up...

What's your FUNCTION?

It feels like *everything* in PHP is a function, yes? I mean, it functions, right? Well, this definition of "functions" is a little bit different.

A FUNCTION in PHP is really quite easy to understand - It is a chunk of code (like a "snippet", if you are familiar with that term) that can be named and reused at any time. Remember earlier when we were talking about repetitive tasks? Functions can help us further reduce these time-killers by writing a block of code once, then defining it as a function. Kinda like a great big variable. Here's how it works:

```
<?php

function MyFunctionName(){

//define your function here

}

?>
```

Functions are quite cool, because they can be considered building blocks of a web application. Let's say you want every page of a website to say your company name.

Let's create a function to do so. Let's call it myCompanyName.

```
<?php
function myCompanyName(){
}
?>
```

Now, let's add the code we want to execute between the curly brackets:

```
<?php
function myCompanyName(){
 echo "Welcome to The Creamy Bagel Company!<br />";
}
?>
```

So now whenever we want our company name to appear, you can call the function within a PHP tag anywhere!

Isn't it about time you experienced a better bagel?
Welcome to The Creamy Bagel Company!

```
<?php
function myCompanyName(){
 echo "Welcome to The Creamy Bagel Company!<br />";
}

echo "Isn't it about time you experienced a better bagel?<br />";
myCompanyName();

?>
```

Output looks like this...

A Function can contain just about any type of PHP code, so I hope you can see how useful this can be - it can definitely be a timesaver when working with a lot of code.

PHP SESSIONS

When your websites start to become more advanced and you find that you have a need for specific user data to be available throughout different pages on your website (think shopping cart!), it's time for Sessions!

Starting a session is a snap.

<?php

session_start();

?>

The webserver will attach a really really long random "session ID" to indicate a unique session. It looks something like: a8486dd2a3eacc136bd44ca653d8c5a2

A session isn't worth a hill of beans unless we can store data in it. Fortunately, PHP can do this for us with an associative array, based on the $_SESSION variable. (Is some of this starting to come together?)

Let's make a login form based on sessions!

```php
<?php
session_start(); //  Starts a PHP session
echo "<form method=POST action=index.php>
  User Name: <input type=text name=\"username\">
  Password: <input type=text name=\"password\">
  <input type=submit>
  </form>";  // This is the HTML form
$_SESSION['username']=$_POST["username"]; // Enters the username into the array
$_SESSION['password']=$_POST["password"]; // Enters the password into the array
?>
```

Your username and password are now stored in an array that will last until the session is "un-set".

Removing a session is done when either: The viewer closes their browser, or PHP runs the command to un-set a session, aka "destroy".

You can think of it like this - your session is an Etch-a-Sketch[tm] that has information drawn on it. It's there until you shake it!

```php
<?php

session_destroy();

?>
```

Yes, it's a tad violent...but gets the job done. This will clear out any data associated with the current session.

So, what if I want to remove specific data from a session without deleting the whole thing?

This can be done with an IF statement combined with commands called "ISSET" and "UNSET".

```php
<?php
if(isset($_SESSION['items'])){
unset($_SESSION['items']);}
?>
```

So, logically...

If this specific *key* is set in this *session*, *remove* the *key's* data.

Cookies (mmmmmm!)

You are hopefully familiar with Cookies - you get them almost anytime you visit a website. Cookies allow you to store information about your visitor's session on their computer.

One of the most common uses of cookies is to store usernames. That way when a viewer returns to your site, they don't have to log in each time they visit.

You can create cookies in PHP with:

```
<?php

setcookie(name, value, expiration);

?>
```

There are 3 requirements when setting a cookie:

- **Name**: This is where you set the name of your cookie so you can retrieve it later.

- **Value**: The value you wish to store in your cookie. Some common values are usernames or date last visited.
- **Expiration**: When your cookie will be deleted from the user's computer. *If you do not set an expiration date, the cookie will be deleted when the viewer closes their browser!*

Getting information from a cookie is just about as easy as setting one. Remember the "ISSET" stuff a few minutes ago? PHP gets cookie data in a similar way, by creating an associative array (Yes, again!) to store your retrieved cookie data...using the $_COOKIE variable. The array key is what you named the variable when it was set (so, obviously you can set any number of cookies!) So... (next page please!)

```
<?php
if(isset($_COOKIE['username'])){ // If there's a cookie...
$username = $_COOKIE['username']; // set the variable...
echo "Welcome back, $username."; // and show the data in the cookie...
} else {
echo "No username was found. Sorry!";} // or show this if there wasn't one.
?>
```

And, FYI...Cookies are stored as small text files on your computer (in case you did not know!)

And now...one of the most useful functions of PHP...

PROCESSING FORMS

What is one thing almost everyone wants to do with their website? Have a contact form. And, it isn't as difficult as you'd think. We're going to use the PHP mail() command to make one.

Make an HTML form with Name, Email and Message fields. Take the code below and place it in a PHP file to use as your action.

```
<?php
mail("myaccount@myisp.com", "Form Feedback", " // your address and subject
Name: $name
Email: $email
Message: $message
", "From: $email");
// Display results
echo("
<html>
Name: $name
Email: $email
Message: $message
</html>
");
?>
```

Section Two Overview

In this section, we covered some more advanced features of PHP. Not for the timid, but not impossible to grasp!

IF - Do something if something is true.
ELSE - Do something else if it isn't
ELSEIF - Add more choices to IF
SWITCH - Use this if you have a lot of ElseIf's
ARRAY - One variable, many values
ASSOCIATIVE ARRAY - One variable, even more values
LOOPS - For, While, For Each - A way to repeat code
FUNCTIONS - Turn a big code chunk into a small one
SESSIONS - Carry unique data from page to page
COOKIES - Store session data on your viewer's computer
FORM PROCESSING - Process web forms, such as a mailer

QUIZ TIME!

1. What are the 3 ways to comment code in PHP?

2. ELSEIF cannot be used without _____

3. What are Cookies used for in PHP?

Section 3:

Oh No - Not MySQL

Covering MySQL connection and basic manipulation through PHP

More Functionality with a database

Nowadays you hardly ever hear PHP mentioned without MySQL close behind. Why? Well, PHP and MySQL make a great pair for web application development efforts. MySQL is often used in conjunction with PHP for the same reasons PHP is so popular - it is free, widely available, and most web hosts have it installed. There are other database systems that PHP works with, but MySQL seems to be the most common.

In this section, I'll familiarize you with using MySQL to connect to a MySQL database and perform the basics. Advanced MySQL and it's SQL language is a little beyond the scope of this book, so we won't dive very far in to heavy details (I don't want to lose you!). However, MySQL's commands are written in almost-plain-english, and you can usually figure it out just by looking at it.

Most other PHP/MySQL books also tell you how to install MySQL and configure it. We're not going to do that here. Your web host most likely has MySQL available for you, and they have simple ways to create databases. The two hosts that I have been using for years are pair Networks and Hostgator. Hostgator uses CPanel, and pair Networks uses a custom built control panel - both make it very easy to set up a database, and they provide the information you need to connect to it with.

So, let's get connected!

Making the connection to MySQL...

First off, we need to be able to tell PHP to connect to a database before we can use it. The command is straight forward - mysql_connect().

```
<?php

$dbhost = "localhost"; // the db's server

$dbname = "mysite_dbname"; // the db's name

$dbuser = "mysite_dbuser"; // the db's username

$dbpass = "password"; // the password for the user

mysql_connect ($dbhost, $dbuser, $dbpass) or die (mysql_error());
//connect to db or show error if failure

echo "Connected to database";
```

?>

Looking at the above code, everything is pretty self explanatory...except the "or die" thing. This is a method of handling errors. If for some reason PHP cannot connect to the database, the "or die(mysql_error())" part tells PHP to show us exactly what the error was. Most of the time it is human error - the wrong username, password, etc. was entered in the code. Check your work!

Putting The *Data* In The *Base*

OK! We're connected to a MySQL database! Far out! Now what? We need to put data IN to the database and use it!

So, here's how we do it.

First of all, you have to select the database with the mysql_select_db() command.

<?php

mysql_select_db("my_db") or die(mysql_error());

?>

Create Tables (and do just about everything else!) with MYSQL_QUERY

Now that we've selected the database we want to use, we need to put some tables in the database in order to store data. Before that happens, though, you need to think about what kind of data is going in to your tables. I'll get to why in a moment. Here's a simple example of table creation with the **mysql_query** command:

<?php mysql_query("

CREATE TABLE Employees

(employee_id INT,

first_name VARCHAR(50),

last_name VARCHAR(50)")

?>

You'll need to define the type of data that is going in to each table field...which is why you'll need to put some thought into your database before you start creating tables.

On the next page lies some common types of data. Remember, if you try to put text (TEXT) into a field that is defined to take numbers (INT), you're going to get errors! (It's the square-peg-round-hole scenario!)

Common Field Data Types:

CHAR() – Fixed length field between 0 and 255 characters that can store any type of data. The length of the field is set regardless of the size of the data placed into it.
DATE – Date in YYYY-MM-DD format.
INT – Whole numbers only. The number of digits can also be specified in parentheses, but is not necessary.
TEXT – Variable length text-only field with a maximum length of 65535 characters.
TIME – Time in hh:mm:ss format.
VARCHAR() – Variable length field between 0 and 255 characters that can store any type of data. Unlike the **CHAR()** type, the length of each **VARCHAR()** field is determined by the data placed into it.

So, knowing this, let's decipher our code example from above.

<?php mysql_query("

CREATE TABLE Employees

(open the query to the DB and make this table with Employees as the name)

(employee_id INT,

(make this field with employee_id as the name and allow only whole numbers)

first_name VARCHAR(50),

(make this field with first_name as the name, allow any input, and limit it to 50 characters in length)

last_name VARCHAR(50)")

(make this field with last_name as the name, allow any input, and limit it to 50 characters in length)

?>

Once you get the basic concepts, data manipulation with MySQL is not difficult. Let's dive in a little bit more to the way tables are laid out.

The Primary Key

Spreadsheet programs (such as Microsoft Excel) have row numbers to identify what row a certain bit of data is in. Databases have a similar identifier, called the *Primary Key*. You can draw out your database with relative ease - or you can create a mock up of it in a spreadsheet. For example:

This is a

Primary Key	employee_id	first_name	last_name
0	101	Bill	Lumbergh
1	102	Tom	Smykowski
2	103	Michael	Bolton
3	104	Peter	Gibbons

Table: Employees

graphical representation of our code example on the previous page. Seems easy when you look at it, right?

How do I remember what the primary key is when I make a new row of data?

When you create the tables, there are going to be more options that you need to include to make your database a little easier to use...specifically being AUTO_INCREMENT and NULL / NOT NULL. First, the code example...

Real World Code Example:

```php
<?php
// Make a MySQL Connection
mysql_connect("localhost", "user", "password") or die(mysql_error());
mysql_select_db("test_db") or die(mysql_error());

// Create a MySQL table in the selected database
mysql_query("CREATE TABLE Employees(
id INT NOT NULL AUTO_INCREMENT,
PRIMARY KEY(id),
 employee_id INT,
 first_name VARCHAR(50),
 last_name VARCHAR(50)")
 or die(mysql_error());

echo "Table Created!";

?>
```

Let's run through this one, step by step.

First, we make a connection to the MySQL database and select the database we want to work on.

Then, we make a table called "Employees", with a column called "id" that will automatically increment by 1 each time a new record is created, has a NOT NULL value (this simply means that the "id" value is real and searchable), and that the Primary Key is set to be the "id" field. Now, we create our three data fields (employee_id, first_name, last_name), and issue the good ol' "or die" command to tell us if something went wrong.

IF NOT EXISTS
Will creating a table that is already in use break a script?

Yes indeedy. Which is why you'll want to use the "IF NOT EXISTS" command with CREATE. This will prevent the table from being created if it exists already. It's horrible english, but can save some frustration!

Note: If this is a *brand new* database that you just created, you won't have to worry about tables existing already. It's just good practice to throw the If Not Exists command in there for when you are adding tables to an *existing* database.

<?php mysql_query("

CREATE TABLE IF NOT EXISTS Employees

(employee_id INT,

first_name VARCHAR(50),

last_name VARCHAR(50)")

?>

The "IF NOT EXISTS" clause can be used for other things in MySQL, such as creating databases. You can use it (and it's partner IF EXISTS) in data selects and other queries as well.

INSERTING DATA

Using the "Employees" example from earlier, here's the syntax on inserting data into a table. *Save Time: use a PHP Function and/or an Include to set up the mysql_connect statement, since it has to exist whenever you to a database.*

<?PHP

mysql_connect (My_DB, user, pass) or die (mysql_error());

mysql_query("INSERT INTO Employees

(employee_id, first_name, last_name) VALUES('103', 'Michael', 'Bolton') ")

or die(mysql_error());

?>

GETTING DATA with SELECT, FROM

Putting data into a table is great. Eventually you're going to have to get data back *out* if you want your web app to be useful! Here's where SELECT and FROM come in handy!

Usage: SELECT something FROM Table

If you wanted to select *everything* from a table, use an *.
Like this: SELECT * FROM Table

Or, you can select specific things by the row's Primary Key.
Like this: SELECT 3 FROM Table

You can also use WHERE to further dig to the data that you want:
SELECT * FROM Table WHERE last_name='Lumbergh'

Let's dive back in to our Employee table, shall we?

<?PHP

mysql_connect (My_DB, user, pass) or die (mysql_error());

mysql_query('SELECT * FROM Employees WHERE last_name="lumbergh"') or die(mysql_error());

?>

Now, what if we couldn't remember how to spell Lumbergh, and just wanted to find employees last names that begin with "L", we can use the % as a wildcard symbol. Like this:

mysql_query('SELECT * FROM Employees WHERE last_name="l%"') or die(mysql_error());

Now, the query will return any data in the last_name field that begins with the letter L.

UPDATING DATA

If data needs to change, we can update it using the UPDATE and SET commands (I know - shocking, isn't it?). Let's pretend Peter Gibbons has changed his last name to Griffin. We'll simply update the field...

<?php

We'll skip the connection, you should have it as a function already!

mysql_query("UPDATE Employees SET last_name='Griffin' WHERE employee_id='104'")

?>

...add a tad of olive oil and some oregano, and the field is changed!

DELETING DATA

Just as we want to add data, there will be times that we need to delete data as well.

<?php

Once again...you should be able to connect by now!

mysql_query("DELETE FROM Employees WHERE employee_id='104'")

?>

...and there you have it!

OK...I won't go any further. I'm sure your mind has had enough for now. I hope this higher level overview of MySQL and how to use it with PHP. There are a LOT more functions available in MySQL, but we won't cover them this time.

Wrapping It Up

Well, that's it! I hope you come away from this book with a good solid understanding of what PHP can do for you. When you first start out, PHP looks intimidating (I know it did to me!), but when you get down to the nitty gritty of it, the most difficult thing about it is remembering the syntax.

Quick PHP Reference

ECHO: Outputs to the screen.
STRING: Content within a PHP command.
VARIABLES: Something equals something else.
DATE: A way to display date/time.
INCLUDE: Pull in the contents of another file.
REQUIRE: Require the contents of another file.
HEADER: Redirects to new file / URL.
IF - Do something if something is true.
ELSE - Do something else if it isn't.
ELSEIF - Add more choices to IF.
SWITCH - Use this if you have a lot of ElseIf's.
ARRAY - One variable, many values.
ASSOCIATIVE ARRAY - One variable, even more values.
LOOPS - For, While, For Each - A way to "loop" through code.
FUNCTIONS - Turn a big code chunk into a small one.
SESSIONS - Carry unique data from page to page.
COOKIES - Store session data on your viewer's computer.
FORM PROCESSING - Process web forms, such as a mailer.

HELPFUL LINKS:
PHP Homepage:
 http://www.php.net
MySQL Homepage:
 http://www.mysql.com
PHP Builder community:
 http://www.phpbuilder.com
PHP Resource (great scripts here!):
 http://php.resourceindex.com

About The Author

Put your bio and links here!

UPDATES and ERRATA

Put your information here

www.ingramcontent.com/pod-product-compliance
Lightning Source LLC
Chambersburg PA
CBHW040918180526
45159CB00002BA/526